Ruža
Dabić-Bučak

Petals

A collection of poetry

First published by Busybird Publishing 2022

Copyright © 2022 Ruža Dabić-Bučak

ISBN:
Print: 978-1-922691-94-1

This work is copyright. Apart from any use permitted under the *Copyright Act 1968*, no part of this publication may be reproduced, stored in a retrieval system or transmitted in any form or by any means, electronic, mechanical, photocopying, recording or otherwise, without the prior written permission of Ruža Dabić-Bučak.

The information in this book is based on the author's experiences and opinions. The author and publisher disclaim responsibility for any adverse consequences, which may result from use of the information contained herein. Permission to use any external content has been sought by the author. Any breaches will be rectified in further editions of the book.

Cover image: Pixabay

Cover design: Busybird Publishing

Layout and typesetting: Busybird Publishing

Editor: Krystle Herdy

Busybird Publishing
2/118 Para Road
Montmorency, Victoria
Australia 3094
www.busybird.com.au

Without petals, there is no rose.

Without the rose, there is no harmony.

Without harmony, there is no love.

To my family, my friends
and all people of goodwill.

With love,
Ruža

CONTENTS

THANK YOU	1
SIXTY	2
TASSIE, HERE WE COME	4
CRO' GANG	5
MIŠKO IS COMPLAINING	6
THIRD DAY	7
OUR GIFT	9
NAN	10
REMEMBER	12
MY AUTUMN	14
MY MEMORIES	16
LILY	18
DEAR MIHOLA AND MARK	20
MONDAY	21
LAMB FROM ŽUPANJA	23
ŽUPANJA	25
MY OLD PLACE	28
NOAH	29
SEE YOU SOON	30
WA	31
LOVE	34
ANA IS 60	35
CHINA 2012	36
LIFE	38
MARA	39
S&P 2013	40
OUR ADRIATIC	42
MIŠKO IS 65	44
GOOD MORNING SLAVONIJA	46
44	47
SUMMER 2013	48
WOUNDED BIRD	49
OLD FRIENDSHIP	50
YOU WILL BE SEVEN	51
TO OUR VOLUNTEERS	52
KRISTINA	53
FIJI 2014	54
TWO BOYS FROM CERNA	55
ABYSS	56

DOES IT? WILL IT?	57
WHERE?	58
WAIKIKI BEACH	59
THUNDER	60
US	61
MARK	62
IT IS SO	63
THE ETERNAL SECRET	65
MY CHILDHOOD	67
MY EARLY YOUTH	71
DOOM NAMED COVID-19	74
ŠEĆERANA'S CHAMPS-ELYSEES AVENUE	76
KOLONIJA ŠEĆERANA WAS, NOW ISN'T	79
ŽUPANJA RAILWAY STATION	83
ŠEĆERANA'S ACACIAS	86
WHO IS A SLAVONIAN?	88
LAPLAND, 2010	90
SNOWY ŽUPANJA	93
IT WAS LIKE THIS. IT STILL IS	96
LILY IN ŽUPANJA	100
THE EXODUS FROM ŽUPANJA	104
ŽUPANJA'S IMMIGRANTS IN MELBOURNE	107
SLAVONIAN NIGHTINGALE	109
PRESERVE THE CROATIAN WORD	111
MY MAMA	114
POOR CHILD'S IRRELEVANCE	117
MY WINTER	119
TUC-TUC	122
TOO LATE	125
THE MAGIC OF LIFE	127
FREEZING AGONY	129
ALONE	130
ŠEĆERANA'S CHRISTMAS, MINE, ONCE UPON A TIME	131
MEMORIES	135
MULWALA LAKE	138
ŽUPANJA'S HOT, HUMID SUMMERS, MINE, ONCE UPON A TIME	140
BOSNIANS ARE PEOPLE	144
CLOSE YOUR EYES	146
R	149
Glossary	151
About the Author	152

THANK YOU

For my long, long gone childhood,
for the closeness of sisterhood.

For the wonderful youth of my life,
full of excitement and lots of strife.

For pride, which they say is a sin,
it often got me through, that and a grin.

For my mother and all her devotion.
Warm memories to fill an ocean.

For, most importantly, my number one,
family and friends and all they`ve done.

For days good and bad
and the mistakes I have made.

For love, life's greatest need,
both given and received.

For today,
from the bottom of my heart,
thank you, I say.

SIXTY

Sixty is a milestone.
In it I am stuck
but is it courage or luck?

From the time of crawling and falling,
the road was long and hidden.
Full of curiosity and learning,
many done deeds were forbidden.

Mirror, mirror, you fickle need,
are you truthful or redeemed?

You are truthful, I am aware,
so do not trick me,
don`t you dare.

Where is my brown hair?
My freshness and tender skin?
That thin waist and my speed?
Oh yes, where indeed?

Look there! It's all gone.
Running away, disappearing
without any shoes on.

I am standing now, asking
how, when and where?
*Ruža, look all around you,
at what is in your love, basking.*

*Your marriage and health,
your family, friends and wealth.
This is love and happiness.
I tell you, this is life's greatest gift.
This is all that matters, if you get my drift.*

My heart and soul know
there is no time to moan,
so I shout,
'Six-Zero, welcome with all my heart!
All questions and shadows
can now depart.'

TASSIE, HERE WE COME

We are going on a trip;
in a holiday fever grip.
On the Spirit, 9 am this morning,
to Tasmania, it`s a warning.

The four Dabić girls,
loving sisters
full of lustre
like Broome pearls.

With Steve and Darko`s fingers missing,
Miško`s knee replaced
and Victor`s ankle bruised,
is anyone amused?
Goodness gracious me!
Why not? We are all family.

Despite Seka`s dodgy heart,
Ana`s crook back
and Ruža and Mira's nasty cough,
we are finally ready to depart.

Dear Tassie, here we come
to your beautiful land.
Full of green hills,
good beer and cheese,
thanks for your welcome hand.

There's a lot to see, I say.
Cataract Gorge, old Ross,
little devils but no tigers.
Hobart town, Wineglass Bay
and else, be as it may.

Should we drink lots of tea?
A lot? Maybe not!
I'd hate to stop for a pee.

CRO' GANG

Our Croatian gang
arrived with a bang
wondering if Tasmanians
will have a problem
with our Cro' slang.

Holy water, well, well.
So much we could tell.
Victor booked a small bus
to fit all eight of us.

Our nominated drivers, Darko and Vic,
got us moving nice and quick.
Destination: Launceston,
led by a dizzy GPS toy.
Did it have us worried? Yes. Oh boy!

We went on and on
through odd places and dark bush.
We questioned every turn
but were told to relax and shush.

Do not shush me,
I am hungry; I've had no food.
A Big Mac is what I need.
Listen, take note indeed.

Round and round we went
on finding it dead bent.

Look there, do not miss!
A Grand Angus and chips.
Dear God, thank you
for this heavenly bliss!

We all ate.
What the heck?
Live long, the good old
Big Mac.

MIŠKO IS COMPLAINING

Miško is complaining
that his knee is sore,
as stiff as a board.
He stops, keeps quiet,
but complains again
like a little boy in pain.

I say, 'Exercise like this.'
He replies, 'It's not easy.'
'I believe it is not,
but do it as before,
please.'

Follow my advice,
my dear.
Good results will come,
I know.
You know it too;
you are wise.

If others don't agree,
they are wrong,
believe you me.

A pill or two
will surely help
to relieve discomfort,
to improve your health.

Heed my advice, and you'll
feel better each day.
Heed my advice, and your
misery will go away.

THIRD DAY

Blue dawn broke.
It's our third day.
Time to go,
be on our way.
Some aren't ready.
Where are they?
What do you say?

Miško said, 'I suffered all night.
Ruža, what am I to do?'
'Take some meds,
it's a new day.
Get ready,
we have to leave.
The others are well,
I do believe.'

Good morning, Hobart city.
We are hungry.
Come on, team.
Let's find some food.
Thank you, Banjo.
No complaints.
We are sated.
We are all elated.

We stopped at Lark Bar,
they'd so much to taste.
For MM's birth,
we found a good bottle
of whisky to unearth.

-1-

We drove through Bicheno
and found Natureworld.
We looked, we observed,
and about the Tasmanian devil
we learnt.
He was beautiful and
now they believed me,
but for themselves
they had to see.

Dear people,
what a wonder,
a pancake
the size of an elephant
like I'd never seen before.
I ate there yonder
with no feelings of guilt.
Surely, a shirt big enough
is going to hide it.

OUR GIFT

Here we are, at the Resort Cape Schanck
after visiting the Peninsula Hot Springs.
I think all of this
almost broke our kid's bank.

The Hot Springs, what a place!
My to-do list is a mile long:
- indulge hunger and thirst
- refresh body and soul
- polish this old love

But what to do first?

Oh dear, oh dear!
We did it all.
Hot baths; Kodo massage;
good food; Red Hill beer.

Once in our room,
I wanted to sleep
but my darling said,
'Let's go for a walk
in the Cape Schanck National Park
to burn some fat
before it gets too dark.'

What a beautiful day.
Happy and content.
Yes, happy but exhausted
after so much play.

NAN

About you I'd heard
long before we met.
You in day oncology,
ruling with an iron word.

I wished to work there,
but 'Nan is too fussy,' I was told.
What did that mean?
Was I not good enough
or perhaps just too old?

With a stroke of fate,
on to that ward I got.
What did you think
about that, mate?

Both of us born
in the sign of a fish.
Dear me,
what a confusing dish.

Two heads, yes,
facing opposite sides.
One brutally direct,
the other loyal and kind.

You worked so hard.
Were you made of stone?
Not your bones, we know.
Your mind? Yes!
But that's the way you were born.

To the Austin you gave
your life and devotion,
if saved up, I bet you
they could fill an ocean.

Chaos filled your NUM room.
To enter it,
one had to fly in on a broom.
Packed from rafters to floor
with things galore,
but Tracey's offer to clean
was refused with a roar.

If anyone sat in your blue chair,
'Get away,' you'd say with air.
You'd tell them to sit in any other
and walk away with a shudder.

'NAN' R. WENDEL COOK,
goodbye, so long, farewell.
My thanks and love to you.
Enjoy your life
soaking in a long, hot bath,
reading a good book.

-2-

REMEMBER

Remember, my love,
all those years ago,
what your wish was,
my then restless dove.

To live in Australia
was your young life's aim;
freedom and opportunity to gain.

To work, to be happy, to live free,
one had to leave the old country,
one had to secretly flee.

You asked me, would I ever?
What? Australia? So far away?
No, not me. No, never.

To go with you towards your aim,
leaving family and friends,
my streets and trees,
my then life,
would cause too much pain.

About this you ceased talking
until we started our married line walking.

When I saw the truth and injustice,
how they boxed us in,
I felt this terrible ache
and knew what I had to forsake.

I changed my mind,
so here we came
to our good life, opportunities to find.

We made a break
for ourselves and our unborn children.
For a much better future to make.

With our first child on the way,
we arrived in March 1971
to a huge place
in Port Phillip Bay.

Oh, there was pain,
heartache and tears.
If saved in a tub,
one could sit in it
up to one's ears.

This beautiful, kind land
gave us opportunities to no end.
To work hard, a decision made
to realise our plans,
we both firmly said.

So we did it. That we did.

Looking back, I see
this is where I wanted to be.
It didn't take me long
to know exactly where I belong.

Our son and daughter are happy
and our gorgeous grandkids are here
with another on the way.
I thank you for giving us a hand,
you blessed sunburnt land.

Now we are here,
content and reflecting.
Great vision, huge dreams.
A decision well made,
my best friend, my dear.

-2-

MY AUTUMN

I am sitting, thinking,
looking at these hands of mine;
beautiful once,
now, much changed with time.

I should scream
for it to get away.
This cruel disaster
to body and mind,
life's certain master.

Thin and straight my fingers were,
thicker with knobs now there.
My wedding ring feels too tight
but is it from age or fright?

Bones aching, joints creaking,
it's so hard to bend.
Can you give us a hand?
What we need is little grease.
Please, arthritis, please.

My hormones flew away
with the winds of youth,
causing so many problems,
and you know that's the truth.

Hot flushes keep me awake,
enough heat to bake a cake.
Doona on, doona off.
Nightie on, nightie off.
What is the deal?
It is all against my will.
I was given medication
by my doctor for salvation.

My skin, once the colour of milk,
no blemishes or blue veins,
and the feel of finest silk,
is now dry and a little loose,

demanding and wanting
of cream, lotion, more cream.
For me, the job is daunting.

Once, the eyesight of an eagle,
sharp and so precise,
helpless without assistance now,
so to my glasses, I take a bow.
Without these faithful helpers,
life would be dark and sad,
full of despair and uselessness,
so heartbreakingly bad.

'Til twenty-six, my hair was brown
but much too early the battle was lost
to this silver-grey crown.
Many love the colour of my hair.
Healthy and shiny, they all say,
but they haven't had it as long as me.
Don't you think
this price is too high to pay?

My body is changing,
there's no escape there.
No, I cannot stop it,
despite constant care.

Some things are better now:
my mind and inner calm,
I've understanding and tolerance,
a very precious balm.

Should I mourn this past of mine?
I could, but I won't.
I am happy and content
with no real reason to pine.

My innocent youth has gone,
the long hot summer, too.
I'm slightly limping,
but wonderful autumn
is saying how do you do?

MY MEMORIES

Today, on the way
to visit your grave,
memories of you
kept coming, Mama,
beautiful and brave.

I remember sitting in a car,
following the hearse,
thinking, begging,
'Please, driver, slow down,
don't drive so fast.
I don't want my Mama
going into the ground
even though she must.'

With the wind, gone
are the last nineteen years.
Time has mellowed pain
and dried away the tears.

You were going, that you knew.
You looked at the doctor and said,
'No chemo. I am not afraid,
but please, no pain.
My decision is made.'

I still miss your gentle touch
and cheating at playing cards;
your cheeky smile and quick step.
You were loved so very much.

During summer picnics,
you had lots of fun
spraying others with water,
then fast away you'd run.

-1-

I am so grateful
you did not suffer long
but went quickly to heaven
where all angels belong.

To help you leave,
I had to make you believe,
from us, here,
to your mama and father,
you're two sons and others
you'd cross over to, my dear.

As if in a doubt, you asked,
'Do you really believe this?'
With all my heart, Mama.
You can do it with ease.

You looked at us, your daughters
and grandchildren, too.
You touched my face
and with a smile,
whispered your last words,
'My beautiful doves.'
You closed your eyes
and went to that heavenly place.

I thought, perhaps I should
put my thoughts to paper,
so that our memories of you
go on and grow forever greater.

-2-

LILY

Beautiful ray of sunshine,
like lightning, you came
after years of my hoping for
the Grandma title to be obtained.

A fairy tale in shades of pink,
your childhood is
one big happy play,
rich enough to fill each day.

Like two pieces of live coal,
your eyes are bright
as priceless beacons
on a stormy night.

Silky soft is your touch.
Your mouth, a tiny cherry.
Our firstborn darling grandchild,
we love you so very much.

Your sweet voice
is a nightingale's song.
Hearing it is a
constant reason to rejoice.

Like a summer sunset,
your hair, copper brown,
sitting on your head
like a shiny crown.

Have you already lived?
Is this your second time here?
You know so much.
To me, it's not too clear.

Love for your Dida
always very great,
there for all to see
'til this very date.

Dida lift me! Put me down!
I want this, maybe that.
Needing, wanting on and on,
all your wishes are promptly met.

Dida's eyes full of plea,
asking, begging anyone,
do come and help me.

'Baka, Baka, look at this!'
'Biscuits, lollies, sweets, please!'
'I love chocolate most, you know!'
With desire, your face aglow.
Your wishes I do hear,
little angel, my darling dear.

'I am not hungry;
don't want dinner.
I don't like this.' Always thinking
you are the winner.

You are our life's need,
like fresh air, food
and warm sun indeed.

Love for your mama—
in the most special bond—
this unreserved devotion
overflowing the biggest ocean.

Our grandchild
loved so dearly.
Why? How? Really?

My beloved child's child.
A wonderful miracle, I say.
Thank you, Chris and Kristina,
for the ultimate gift in every way.

Lily Dabić-Bučak-Guest,
our perfect, round pearl,
born of love, to be loved,
you most precious little girl.

-2-

DEAR MIHOLA AND MARK

Fast approaching is the day
when MM is going to
knock on the door and say,
'Mama, please let me out.
I want to see you and Tata.
I want to loudly cry,
to demand all the attention.
I want lots of kisses and cuddles
and a great big reception.'

Soon I'm to be a grandma again.

MONDAY

Monday is a special day.
If you ask why,
and you may,
I'll tell you,
it goes this way.

Long before Lily's birth,
at work, I asked
for an extra day
to devote to a grandchild
when one came to this earth.

Lucky me, I got both,
Mondays and a grandchild.
Ever since then,
Lily and I do as we like,
what, where and when.

By doing that,
my daughter has free time
and Lily is happy
with people who love her.
So many needs are met.

Baka Mimi lives near.
We go to see her.
She always has sweets
and to Lily, she's very dear.

Baka Ana is on our list,
so to Williamstown we visit.
With black swans to feed,
we're doing a good deed.

-1-

Sometimes we have a date
with Tomas and Lara
in Glenroy. Not far away
to have a good time and play.

Baka Seka is not forgotten,
especially in summer
when strawberries are ripe
and they slide nicely
down Lily's pipe.

We also have a strawberry patch.
Very small indeed
but it keeps Lily supplied,
so it's really all we need.

Our strawberries grow fast
with Dida's *magic touch*.
From Coles fruit shelves
to our garden,
thank you very much.

Lily picks them with delight
and no suspicion at all,
that is 'til we are discovered,
'til our fib comes to light.

Lily loves water like a little fish.
Many mornings are spent
at Mill Park indoor pools
to grant her this wish.

My life is very, very good.
I am so blessed, I have so much
that I never thought I would.

-2-

LAMB FROM ŽUPANJA

1958 was an important year.
A gorgeous baby arrived
in Županja,
the heart of my Slavonija,
like a shooting star,
to all very clear.

That warm day
in the month of May,
a baby was born.
Fourth girl child,
to our father's scorn.
To mama and us,
a pure delight,
I say.

She was given the name Marija
by our mother,
but from the very beginning,
she was simply Mira.
To us, a very good idea.

She was so cute
despite being bald,
but soon her hair grew
curly, blond and thick,
as soft as the finest silk.

Mira was naughty only once.
Moved a chair from
underneath our mum
and received a good smack;
her first and last one.
Our neighbour Pišta
called her a little doll.
She was so pretty
and so very small.

-1-

Always as gentle as a lamb,
so we gave her the nickname
Lamb from Županja town,
by which she is now renowned.
Helpful, caring, also kind.
Always thinking of others.
The word angel often
comes to mind.

Years have passed
so very fast,
but my life is happier
with her in it.
A fact that's not hard to admit.

Marija 'Mira' Mimi Dabić,
we love you.
Don't ask why
this is so.
We simply do.

-2-

ŽUPANJA

Županja, Županja.
I am back.
Cradle of my
childhood and early youth,
life's supreme gift to me,
one I treasure always, happily.

The bullet train
named Memories
is taking me back
to the fifties and sixties,
to Slavonija and the Sava river,
causing me to smile and shiver.

It was easy to be happy
with no money or gold,
most of us had none,
making true friends,
young then,
now old.

I had youth and health,
a good mind, innocence
and hope for better days.
Perhaps not soon,
but I knew
they would come
in many different ways.

Šećeranka[1] is what I was
and Kolonija where I lived.
My childhood
and early youth spent there
leaving me
deeply rich with memories.

---

1   A female who lives in the estate Kolonija Šećerana

To the scent of lilac
I grew up and dreamt.
In Kristal Cinema, I discovered movies.
To *La Paloma*[2] I danced.
Through Kolonija I strolled
whether in heat, rain or snow.

Dubravka, Anica, Marija and Rosa,
were my very first childhood friends
during times long gone
when often I ran
with no shoes on.

At our primary school *Boris Kidrič*,
we battled and learnt
to read and write.
We formed friendships
lasting right.

Nada and Josip Barišić,
Jasna and Ivan Herman,
Marija Žigić, Paula Vukašinović,
Radojka Barbir.
Noble people,
true teachers, so very loved.
After forty-five years,
remembered,
deeply respected.

I loved knowledge,
absorbed everything like a sponge.
Often confused, wondering
why, how and what?
Only to realise,
it was all life's plot.

---

2   The name of a song

Political systems were unjust.
People allocated
to sections in life.
Smart but poor into the lower.
The not-so-bright but privileged
closer to the sun and success.
This was to be expected, I guess.

In my allocation,
fate intervened.
Rade Pavlović[3], a good man,
lent me a hand,
unlocking the door
to brighter days,
but left it to me
to find needed ways.

Županja, that part of time,
both yours and mine,
is woven together
into a beautiful picture
as proof of
you and me
in one moment of history.

Županja, please be kind.
Give me a white Christmas
and a magical New Year's Eve, too.
Please make my dream
finally come true.

Although I live happily
far, far away,
you are often in my dreams.
I gladly return to see you and say,
'Županja, How are you?
Good morning. Good day.'

---

3   CEO of the town's sugar factory

MY OLD PLACE

In thoughts every day,
in dreams every night,
to see you one more time,
desire has burning might.

Many years have gone by.
Life carved its way
but feelings for you live on
like thirst, like hunger.
Seeds sown when one was
innocent and young, I say.

Life was a fickle sea.
One day calm, full of promise,
the next, stormy and dark,
flogged by wind,
causing a lasting mark.

'Why have such a strong pull?'
I ask often.
Perhaps I know.
I departed. I left you.
I take responsibility in full.

Time has given me all:
peace, contentment,
prosperity and happiness.
But a glow for you smoulders
today and forever
in the depths of my soul.

NOAH

At 3:26 this afternoon,
a little bright angel
in the form of a baby boy,
much desired and precious,
entered this world
to our greatest joy.

The name Noah he was given
by his loving parents
in the hope that his life is
happy and value-driven.

Many tears were shed
of relief and gladness.
No more waiting in suspense.
All is well, might I add.

Noah is my great delight.
I wish to hold him, touch him,
look at him forever,
such is this baby's might.

The world is richer now,
more beautiful and bright
because this tiny baby
brought his dazzling light.

The delicate fruit of the great love
between my son and a gorgeous woman.
The blood of my blood,
a masterpiece well done.
Thank you, Mihola and Mark,
for giving me my first grandson.

SEE YOU SOON

It's not the length of your stay
but the imprint you leave behind
that counts and lasts
now and forever, I find.

If we could go back in time,
I would change so much.
I'd remove distrust and stress,
start with patience and more of such.

We live and learn,
make mistakes, err,
but most importantly,
a good person loves
and respect they earn.

You will not physically be here,
yet in so many ways,
in all that you have done,
you'll always be near.

Wherever you go,
whatever you do,
hold your head high,
know we will think of you.

As we part today,
not with tears but a smile,
see you soon, we'll say.

WA

Tell me about WA,
you might say.
I cannot,
but I am here
to see, feel, learn
in whichever way.

Nature's gift, the river Swan,
most beautiful at early dawn.
A valuable jewel in Perth's crown,
a playground for boats
bobbing up and down.

We are again on an APT tour
where most people are demure and mature.
Wildflowers we are hoping to see.
It has been wet and cold,
so it is a maybe, maybe.

Took a cruise on the river Swan
down to Fremantle Port,
home to the America's Cup
when it was won.

Stopped at Leeuwin Estate,
we were given wine to taste.
If it was good or not
is still up for debate.

Surely we must be forgiven
for not knowing
when such small sips
were given.

-1-

Ah, the Jewel Cave,
a not to be missed place.
These nature's wonders
look like exquisite lace.

We saw a whale, a southern right,
in Albany's harbour,
showing off its might,
posing for my camera,
making me happy and bright.

We went to Stirling Rangers
with wildflowers still to find.
Some are so very small.
Watch your step,
if you do not mind.

Coolgardie, a quiet and dry town,
like many others,
once famous and rich,
now on riches well down.

Gold made the town's heart beat,
fever and reason refused to meet,
but happiness gave in to despair.
Now it's all gone. Why? Where?

Kalgoorlie is still fine,
so much gold still there
giving it enough shine.

Wave Rock, you old spot,
so calm and peaceful.
Known around the world.
A very important Hyden stop.

-2-

The first inland town of York,
its buildings preserved so well.
Avon River, full of water,
its breathtaking views
inviting me for a long walk.

New Norcia, now a quiet place,
founded and built by Spanish monks,
is still so rich and full of grace.
Monkey Mia it is called,
nicely nestled in Shark Bay,
home to dolphins, dugongs,
sharks, sea turtles and more.
What a unique part of the world.

What we did next is a must!
Walk along Shell beach,
visit Hamlin Pool,
pay homage to ancient stromatolites
and learn about the past.

Pinnacles, what an eerie display,
like limestone fairies
waiting on ready
with wind and sand to play.

This is an experience of mine.
I saw, felt and learnt.
I am much wealthier now,
so, enough for this time.

To the wonderful WA
and Jeff and Terry,
our newfound friends,
thank you, I wish to say.

-3-

LOVE

It cannot be stolen or bought
nor forced or earned.
It arrives freely, unplanned.
At times, suddenly like lightning.
At times, quietly and slowly.
Why? How? Often I ask.
To explain it is an impossible task.

With invisible shackles,
enslaved we are,
happily following,
never asking how far.

It enters the heart and mind
without permission,
to quicken our step and breath,
to make us sing and dance,
often leaving us quite blind.

What is this wonderful force?
Magic and tender today,
tomorrow not the same,
yet still desired and much needed.
Love. Love is its name.

The real one stays forever,
shielding us from pain and fear
'til our last breath,
'til our very death.

Regardless of age,
young or old,
we all love,
we are all on the same page.

If you agree, and I hope you do,
without uncertainty,
just say, 'I love you!'

ANA IS 60

Your special day is here
and though
perhaps not desired,
there is nothing for you to fear.

Time has moved fast,
one might say,
like an express train
rushed from station to station,
and on reaching stop 60,
we know, continue it must.

This new journey is promising.
This new journey is bright,
full of peace and joy.
I feel that I know I am right.

You are thoughtful and kind,
loved and nice to have near.
So, have a happy birthday,
my sister, our dear.

CHINA 2012

What a surprise, a pleasant one.
Beautiful Beijing, old and new,
Tiananmen Square, Forbidden City,
Great Wall of China, Copy Market and else.
All visited, well done.

In Xi'an, the old capital,
there were terracotta warriors
for us to find,
right in the centre of China,
if you do not mind.

The Yangtze, the mother river,
lifeline for many,
vital to creatures great and small.
Cruising on Victoria Anna,
we had a great time,
we really had a ball.

Chengdu, a special spot,
unique giant panda
made you a known dot.
Its famous colours of black and white
are known to many
who work hard to keep
its future safe and bright.

Giant Buddha, very old,
the largest and tallest in the world.
Huge attraction, holy.
To Leshan, it's pure gold.

Silk so smooth, gentle to the touch.
So difficult to make,
no wonder it costs so much.

Guilin is a magical place
with Reed Flute Cave
like beautiful fine lace.
Li River, an emerald snake,

mountain peaks on each flank,
proud and stiff, touching the sky,
a gorgeous tapestry you do make.

Next was Suzhou City,
Venice of the East.
Known for culture and gardens,
famous for the weaving of silk,
it really is so very pretty.

We came to Shanghai
to see the Bund, the museum,
Pudong district and Yuyuan Bazaar.
We wanted to experience the
magnetic Maglev train
and eat hot pot.
Shanghai, you are true to your fame.

Lots of people got sick,
both upstairs and down,
leaving us washed out and in sad nick.

I arrived with an open mind,
gained experienced and learnt.
I can eat yoghurt now
and even drink green tea.
This visit was worth it to me.

Our tour director Jay,
a most professional man,
the best of the best
leading a great group of people.
Indeed very lucky,
I really must say.

China, I am glad I came
to say, 'How do you do?'
You made me happy,
so I thank you.

LIFE

Life goes on, day by day,
never asking if it may.
One glides happily like a kite;
the next can hurt with all its might.

Life is fickle, we do know,
like an archer with a bow.
For love and peace we all yearn,
yet we suffer, hurt and burn.

Which arrow will you get?
I think both, do not fret.
Like a ball, it throws one
from ecstasy to heartache,
from despair to hope,
until it's bored, until it's done.

You make your own way,
they do say.
I'd like to disagree;
most are marked in your destiny.

Time works hard
as an artist with a knife.
A nick here, a cut there,
a scrape here, a polish there.
All to create a unique piece
like yours, his, or my life.

Happy or not,
we walk the line.
At times limping,
getting or giving help,
until our own final dot.

MARA

This hot summer morning
at five am on the dot,
Mark and Mihola, again,
Dad and Mum became.

At the crack of dawn,
in the arms of the rising sun,
this baby girl came,
beautiful and healthy.
Thank you, dear Lord,
for this wonderful gain.

To my surprise and great delight,
she was named Mara.
Mara is my mama's name.
It is great, it is very right.

This little, sweet one,
our third grandchild,
desired, welcome and loved,
gives us much happiness and fun.

When I watch her, I smile.
When I nurse her, I am content.
This is a feeling of pure delight;
magic, precious and full of might.

Blood is not water, they say,
which explains our love.
Hope and wishes for the future,
good health and happiness
to you, Mara, our darling little dove.

S&P 2013

I am glad we came
to stunning Portugal
and beautiful Spain.
It went like this—
but forgive me
if there's something I miss.

What did I expect?
I do not know.
I saw, learnt, and experienced much,
ate good food,
drank great wine and such.

Their history is very rich;
some buildings are 500 years old.
Great wealth,
precious, historic gold.

Jorge, our tour director,
who we called George,
did an excellent job
managing and directing
our colourful mob.

Our tour group was
like an international dish:
New Zealanders, Americans, Canadians,
and South Africans, but mostly Aussies,
each adding flavour to the mix.
For better or more
one could not wish.

Heleder, the bus driver,
what can I say?
Poultice for tired eyes.
For getting our bus
through such narrow spaces,
we'd salute him if we may.

Visiting Fatima was such pure delight.
Hearing mass, receiving communion,
for me, the ultimate highlight.

The icing on the cake
was the sound of La Paloma
and Miško by my side.
Oh yes, it was all
very easy to take.

Thank you, adios,
you magical old world.
Stay proud forever.
You treated me well,
to others, this I will tell.

OUR ADRIATIC

Our beautiful sea.
The bluest of the blue.
The clearest of the clear.
Shimmering, calm magic
sent to us from above,
gifted to my people
with love.

How can it be
as blue as the sky,
with rocks so familiar and dear
like silky, soft air?
I really don't know
but it's all so easy to bear.

Lying on the beach,
swimming and admiring.
Never enough
for body and soul.
Very poetic.
Very inspiring.

When I swim, it's magic,
it's like a fairy tale.
I feel warmth and safety,
just like my mum's hug,
just like a bug in a rug.

Seagulls rest on the water,
dip in and serenade their prey,
begging, 'Please come up my way.'

The hot sun and I aren't friends.
It is attractive.
It works very hard,
heats, charms and burns,
but not me!
I choose deep shade
away from its harms.

Andrew and Linda,
like two dolphins,
are forever swimming and diving
while at other times, they're happy
simply joyfully sunbaking.

It's no surprise that
Selin and Zelich couples
spend every summer here.
They have found heaven,
to all that's very clear.

Ivica and Mara,
two halves of one Slavonian couple,
love the sun and the sea.
Here they are relaxed and free.

Even Miško is enjoying
this perfect life,
relaxed and happy,
not counting hours.
Such are the Adriatic's powers.

Me, white Ruža,
sitting, listening and watching
this great expanse
of sapphire blue water,
looking to the heavens with
thanks from your Croatian daughter.

-2-

MIŠKO IS 65

To complain or to celebrate
is the question of today.
Where has he been?
What has he experienced?
It's not hard to say.

'I want to celebrate!' Miško said.
'This full and rich life,
these great memories
I wish to share.
But perhaps not all,
I think I should add.'

In his early youth,
an idea was born;
already in his little head,
the notion to speak the truth.

In 1971, a time long gone,
he flew overseas, far away,
leaving Slavonija's flat fields,
the land where he was born.

He wanted to work hard
and make a good life
for himself and his family.
All were achieved successfully.

-1-

Miško, thank you for your vision.
Many happy lives are
the result of your decisions.

Yours and my blood
through our children
and grandchildren flow.
The river of honesty and love
aimed to a good future.
Only time will show.

I know you're content,
this you've told me.
With your life, you're exactly
where you wish to be.

Dear Miško,
happy birthday!
New knees, a long life,
endless love and much more
are the wishes sent to you
from this hungry crew.

GOOD MORNING SLAVONIJA

Good morning Slavonija,
my proud land.
I am back again
to stand in your flat fields.
Such are my wishes, my needs.

Spain, Portugal, Italy,
Zagreb and the blue Adriatic are great,
but most precious
is mother Slavonija
who is waiting patiently
with a deep yearn
for her child to return.

There is rustling
in the walnut tree canopies;
thick oak forests;
corn and wheat fields;
sugar beet and sunflowers,
and the taste of dust.
In Slavonija, all are a must.

The river Sava flows east,
winding towards its estuary.
Water is life.
The Sava is the water empress,
Slavonija's greatest.

Slavonija's tamburas sounds
play at your heartstrings,
making you jump,
dance and sing.
Such is the joy they bring.

Slavonija lives, gives, remembers.
She tucks away memories,
past and present,
for a better tomorrow.
Slavonija, it will come
with magic rays
of the rising sun.

44

After forty-four years
of marriage,
so many days and nights,
problems and happiness,
we are here again,
at a place we had to leave then.

You are my light and air,
my music and dance,
my support when weak,
my protective shield
against the wind.

A long time has passed,
full of warmth, excitement
and, of course, some storms.
Hard work and success
has brought us to today
from very far away.

We've enriched the world,
I believe,
created our own line,
one that is different and fine.

I loved you yesterday.
I will love you tomorrow.
Today's love will grow more
by the next break of dawn,
and so on and on.

SUMMER 2013

It arrived.
It passed.
More beautiful than a dream.
That desired European summer,
exciting and hot to the extreme.

Oh, it was wonderful.
Melancholic sounds of fado.
Passionate flamenco dances.
Slavonian flat fields.
The Adriatic's crystal blue water.
Slovenia's scenic lakes.
Bosnia's proud green hills.
All European beauties.

To feel Fatima's spirit.
To defeat Međugorje's[4] sharp rocks
up to Apparition Hill.
To stand in Picasso's birth house.
Great food, coffee and wine
hide many spells.
There is something appealing,
something healing.

It's not the shine
nor the material worth
but the people around you
who make heaven on earth.

---

4 A town in Bosnia and Hercegovina

WOUNDED BIRD

Forgive me, wounded bird,
for your sorrow and pain.
The cause is my thorn
but you made a mistake
and became forlorn.

For my flower's nectar,
you have constant hunger
but rushing towards me,
you were careless
and failed to see.

The thorn is a part
of my rose bush,
its duty is to avert
from my delicate flowers
any possible hurt.

In haste,
you put your foot wrong.
For what occurred,
you blamed me,
you silly little bird.

My flower needs you
like food, water and dew,
like the light of the day,
sent from heaven
my way.

Without your voice,
my flower has no scent.
Without your touch,
my flower will not open.
Without your look,
my flower won't be happy.

So, my beloved bird,
heal quickly, please.
Take off and fly
this way to me.

OLD FRIENDSHIP

Conceived and born in childhood.
Grown and fortified in youth.
Given and taken often.
Survived a half of a century.
Travelled millions of kilometres.
Still alive.

Like us, older
but not weaker.

Acquaintances come and go.
Important to some
but not to me.
They are transient flashes in time.

Real friendship
is something else.
It lasts.
It does not tire.
It is not demanding.
It is giving and understanding.

It doesn't care for distance or time.
It sits in your heart and soul.
It cannot be extinguished.
Its small flame glows.
Friends like that are few
in my view.

YOU WILL BE SEVEN

Go to sleep, little darling.
Sweet dreams, good night.
You'll wake up in the AM
rested, fresh and bright.

Tomorrow is your birthday.
You'll be seven years old.
You are a big girl now,
by many you'll be told.

You will never be too old
for us to hug, to kiss,
to spoil, or to love,
our brown-eyed dove.

A year has gone,
our precious little one.
In that short time,
there's much you have done.

You learnt fast:
reading, writing,
playing piano and chess.
You won a gold medal,
spoke some Chinese and Croatian.
You are smart, say this I must.

So, have a happy birthday,
one filled with laughter, joy,
great times, kisses and much play.

TO OUR VOLUNTEERS

Thank you for your unselfish deeds;
your kind words and warm smiles;
the great cups of coffee and tea;
your gentle touch and given hope.
You are everything our patients need.

I am grateful for everything you do.
May you all be blessed
with health, happiness and wealth.

KRISTINA

It cannot be broken or changed,
disqualified or erased.
It is eternal.
It is the parent-child link.
Unequalled in every way,
don't you think?

Even when we are long gone,
it will last through you, our love,
our first born dove.

Your birth left me dazed,
exhausted in sweet pain.
I was never, ever the same again.

Life changed with your birth.
It brought us much happiness,
an exquisite feeling of belonging,
a most desired feeling on earth.

Many years have flown by,
full of excitement and fun.
Through clouds, wind and rain,
lots of hard work,
ending in a huge gain.

You have woven your own nest
with love and success.
You created your own link,
cute, sweet, the best.

You shine more than a pearl.
You are tougher than a diamond.
You are our pride and joy.
We love you now and forever,
our daughter, our beautiful girl.

FIJI 2014

To you, Fiji, we came back,
to your beautiful land
to celebrate our marriage.
The trip so happily planned.

Twenty years ago, we were told
by a gardener on Castaway Island,
'God gave us this land,
our life, this pure gold.'

We love Fijian people
with their gorgeous smiles,
their leisurely walk,
their own Fijian time.
Fiji, your pristine beaches
all go on and on,
I am sure for many miles.

Your waters are crystal clear.
Your white sand, soft and light.
Your songs, full of emotion,
always sung with pride and still devotion.

We were here on a Blue Lagoon Cruise,
twenty years ago
for our 25th wedding anniversary.
Since then, a lot has happened.
We have all changed.
I've more silver hair
and the occasional bruise.

Fiji, it is nice to see you,
to enjoy your company again.
To mark our 45th wedding anniversary
and to say, *How do you do*?

TWO BOYS FROM CERNA

In the charming village of Cerna[5],
on the bank of the river Bosut,
grew two boys:
Ivica one,
Miško the other.
Both named by their beautiful mother.

Their childhood was rough.
So much to do
before and after school.
They coped.
They were tough.

Doing chores alone
or as a team,
each in deep thought,
dreaming his own dream.

Time went by
in school and at work,
at play and sport,
settling many battle scores,
wins and losses,
and a few emotional storms.

They grew into young men,
different but close.
With friends their days were spent
until separated by fate.
To each other they said goodbye,
sadly, with a deep sigh.

Life opened many doors.
Dreams did come true.
Success was achieved.
Love and happiness found.
Both became great fathers.
Two friends.
Two brothers.

---

[5] A village and a municipality in eastern Croatia

ABYSS

You can plan all you want
when you wake up in the morning.
Life has other surprises,
not wished or needed,
yet we have to accept them.
So, do not ask too much,
I say. No, please don't.

I did not see it coming
but it came at me:
humiliation, aching chest,
nausea and the rest.

It went for my mind,
leaving me confused and in pain,
wandering the darkness,
asking, *Why*?
But the answer I could not find.

I usually give, happier helping others,
but in that moment last night,
a calm hand touched me
and taught me to receive.

So, dear angel,
thank you for your deed,
for your guiding light
in my hour of grave need.

DOES IT? WILL IT?

Does evil win? I ask.
Yes, it does,
many would say.
Why, why?
Because it wears a false, attractive mask.

Be good, I was taught
by my mama, by my church.
I fought temptation and shine
to stay on the straight and narrow,
to have pain and heartbreak brought.

How do I heal my broken heart?
How do I find peace of mind?
How do I walk through a stormy night?
Towards calm waters,
Towards a sunrise, warm and bright?

Snap out of it!
I tell myself,
but the words do not stick.
Perhaps time is what I need
to rebuild myself brick by brick.

When evil shuts its dark eyes
for some rest and a good night,
may the dart of justice
find that it is right.

WHERE?

You may ask,
where has my sunshine gone?
But I don't know.
Suddenly it left you,
away it has flown.

You can't hear the rustle of the sea.
You can't see the beauty of the tree.
You can't hear birds singing.
There are only muffled bells ringing.

You know your way,
perhaps rocky, grey and hard.
Do not fear;
The power of mighty love
will always be near.

One day, my dear,
you will send the rain away.
You will send the clouds away.
Then, a beautiful blue sky and
your lost sunshine will reappear.

WAIKIKI BEACH

Blue skies,
fluffy white clouds,
clear turquoise, warm water,
sand as fine as icing sugar.

People of all ages
rest in the shade,
though many do not.

Waves gently caress the shore,
again and again and…
never tiring.

The waves don't see the fuss
nor the magic that I see.
They think, *'This is simply
what we do. We play,
always and forever.
Every single day.'*

THUNDER

That look.
Those words.
Distancing, pulling away.

Where did it come from?
Has it been smouldering?
One has to think
it has.

Very sad.
Well, well.
Perfect hit bullseye.
One old heart shattered.
My dear, I don't understand.
Why?

Pain in me.
Dark cloud around me.
I am at a loss.
How do I reach thee?

US

Oh, how young we were
on that rainy day,
year one-thousand nine-hundred sixty-nine.
So long ago, when so happily
we boarded the train of marriage
and went on our way.
Journey: life together.
Destination: unknown.

I was nineteen; you were twenty-one.
Both of us so very keen.
Some disagreed,
thinking us just a touch too green.

We travelled the world.
Fast, slow, fast again.
Through excitement, clouds,
some rain, occasional thunder,
beautiful light, warmth, happiness,
laughter and much wonder.

At train stations, different people came.
Our children and grandchildren,
family and relatives,
friends and others.
Some left, I must say,
but many stayed 'til this very day.

We are here.
Let's celebrate our moment.
Not five days.
Not five months.
Fifty golden years
which deserves some cheers.

How? you ask.
What is our secret source?
Answering that is an easy task.
Then and now,
our love was, and is, an
almighty driving force.

MARK

That early spring morning,
I told them you were coming.
No, not yet. Not due.
But you defied them.
You came.
Oh, what a view.

You, a precious bundle of joy.
Hair the colour of gold,
eyes a chocolate brown.
My adorable baby boy.

Skin velvet soft,
so amazing to touch.
Tiny, perfect mouth.
How lucky I was
to be given so much.

Your trademark is your smile.
It lights up the darkness
and soothes stormy days.
It's seen from afar,
from distances
as great as a mile.

You entwined your family
and created your bloodline.
New sparkling diamonds,
unique and very, very fine.

You are so lovable.
You are so kind.
When I think of you,
these two words
come to mind.

To be with you is fun.
You are generous and loyal.
You make our life complete.
We'll love you forever,
our boy, our son.

IT IS SO

You are too busy to see me.
You are too busy for me to see you.
We all did the same when young.
Humans do it well.
It is nothing new.

Once needed, now not.
Why does it hurt so?
I love you more.
I need you more.
It goes around.
Touches us all.
I know.

Time is ongoing.
Does not sit still.
Today is.
Tomorrow is nil.

This is a poignant story
of a parent and a child,
well-known by all
but hard to take
in its prickly glory.

What can a parent do?
Wait and hope
for their child to find the time?
What to do?
I haven't got a clue.

How do we change the pattern?
We cannot.
We will not.
We do not learn.

So, the young rush
through busy days,
towards this same stage,
this yearning haze.

I know this phenomenon.
It repeats itself,
though I'd rather it not.
Loneliness goes on,
waiting for a brighter dawn.

Busy youth yesterday.
Lonely aged today.

THE ETERNAL SECRET

I have been thinking:
life has gone on forever.
It will tomorrow,
with or without me.
'Til when?
That is the eternal secret.
Will it be solved?
Never.

A candle named life
is lit for everyone.
From our first breath,
it burns,
slowly for some,
fast for others,
but still, it burns
'til our own death.

Like it or not,
rich or poor,
you can't choose.
The hand is dealt.
The servant Yerney[6] would shout,
'Finally, justice! Hurrah!'

What imprints will I leave behind
between my first and last breath?
I think that decision is mine
but I will never know
and think that is fine.

-1-

---

6   A character in a book by Ivan Cankar

The last breath, gentle or not,
will douse my flickering flame.
No more me.
The end came.

On my last journey,
I'll glide over Slavonija
and Županja, too,
for one last look and to say,
'Farewell, and thank you!'

Where to then?
Is it up or down?
If I am asked,
to wherever I can read,
write and dance,
indeed.

-2-

MY CHILDHOOD

During the fifties,
Kolonija Šećerana was
my whole child world,
a place to experience and behold.

Our apartment was great.
We had running water,
a bathroom and toilet,
a wood or coal stove,
electricity and a small radio.
It was in the most beautiful estate.

I had my mother and sisters
and plenty of hugs and kisses.
I had the lot,
I'd thought.

My advanced mama taught me
about tenderness, honesty,
hard work and pride.
Other things were school taught, of course.
A lot I learnt
by observing and listening,
but books were always
my most loyal source.

Money has power,
I knew that early.
We had none,
so for me,
that battle was won.

Friendships, play and learning,
those wonderful nature's gifts.
My imagination, my mind,
my pride and defiance,
all free and needed
for self-reliance.

Why desire lollies
when I had bread and dripping?
Ideal for body,
excellent for soul.
Chocolate, biscuits and oranges
were only a dream that
once a year came true,
a gift to each child,
Father Christmas supplied.

I was very small,
struggled with my school bag.
My name was made diminutive,
of my size it was indicative.

Our lanes, our neighbourhood,
our front and back yards,
all ideal for games of dodgeball,
hide and seek,
hopscotch and tag.
Run, run, run.
We never had enough fun.

Not many of us had a ball,
so, if you had one,
you were the top gun.
To make a mud cannon—
the loudest and the best—
you had to be different,
better than the rest.

I never had a toy
bought from a shop.
I made my own doll;
face from a white rag,
mouth, nose, hair,
eyes a beautiful blue,
all drawn by ink pen.
For me,
that was normal then.

I will never forget
skipping ropes, hula-hoops,
bare feet and open fields;
sorrel, nettle, natural ponds,
canals, tadpoles,
snowdrops and pussy willow
as soft as a silky pillow.

If we wanted an adventure,
we went to the grove
to look for Perica Tamburica's[7]
summer shack.
We never found it
but never stayed long.
We knew what we did was wrong.

Ah, snow, that magic.
We'd wait and whisper
to Saint Catherine
to please bestow
on us that beautiful,
brilliant snow.

After it fell,
screams and squeaks of happiness.
You did not mind
if your big toe peeked
through your gumboot's hole,
begging, 'Let's go home. Save my soul.'

Kindergarten was there
but not for my sort.
Its beauty was well known
but, to me, unknown.

Playground swings,
seesaws, carousels,
all kids' dreams
behind locked gates.
They could not stop my team.
We had a secret passage
through a hedge, under a wire fence
of which we took advantage.
Very early, I realised

---

[7] The name of a local vagrant

that knowledge is food
every day to be pursued.
Many of my words are strange
to today's youth,
but so are theirs to me,
to tell you the truth.

I was taught about
Hungarianisation,
but Croatians today
should learn
about Anglicisation.
Which one is better?
I'd say none.

When all is said and done,
the grass is not always
greener over yonder.
Our Croatian words
are pure wonder.

My precious Kolonija Šećerana,
once perfectly divine,
due to greed,
is facing a sad decline.
Though nothing can change
the beauty of that time,
one thing is still so clear:
those memories will always be mine.

No, they can't be bought,
though I doubt anyone would.
This is personal.
It is my wealth.
It is my childhood.

-4-

MY EARLY YOUTH

Throughout the sixties,
Kolonija Šećerana, Županja
was a special place.
The garden of my early youth,
the start of my future days.

Early youth, bud of my life
full of innocent ignorance.
I had naivety and strong will
to discover the hidden path
of my life and
my time to fulfil.

You look at this bud
and ask yourself,
What does it hide?
It's full of promise and expectation
but nothing is sure.
Any opinions are premature.

Before the bud opens,
you wonder,
will it be white, red or yellow?
Perhaps a yet non-existent blue?
Very desired when starting new.

Air, light, love and food
are needed by all flowers.
One and all,
we need to provide
for the growth of a child.

-1-

*Is the flower going to have
beauty and a scent?
Are things unknown?*
Each flower is elegant.
Each child is delicate.
Great flowers can be found
in even the poorest garden.

My primary school
was a warm nest.
I had it all:
great teachers and friends;
drama group and choir;
girl and boy scouts.
Boris Kidrič, I take my hat off to you
for being the best.

Music and dance,
my early loves,
are still in me
sixty-years later and
practised at every chance.

The sound of the band Kristal.
Tadija's romantic voice.
That restaurant.
The elegant dance hall.
Everything needed by body and soul.

The country club
on Mlaka's corner
was the local music hub.
It had a different ambience,
the sound of the tambura and
plenty of song and dance.

-2-

Why desire the Adriatic
when I had the river Sava?
With famous beaches like Poloji
ideal for summer swimming,
I had no need to complain.

Cinemas showed me
early life and so much more.
They presented a world I could only
deep in my soul long for.

My friendships were important,
could not be bought or forced.
Like love, they were conceived
and born to last
because a friend that is a real one
is a friend that can't be undone.

Long gone is this time of discovery,
of early learning and excitement.
Though there were disappointments,
I am grateful for the happiness.
The time of my early youth
will always remain priceless and ageless.

-3-

DOOM NAMED COVID-19

It came from far away.
From China, some would say.
Invisible but mighty,
sowing its dim seed,
a very dark seed indeed.

A virus from the Corona family,
COVID-19 it was named.
Soon the cause of a great pandemic,
the prince of destruction
title it claimed.

Feeding on our breath,
its aim: chaos and death.
Lives fall like withered petals
through sickness, confusion and fear.
You'd think you can feel it near,
but it is only an illusion.
We can only be certain
when its ugly face does appear.

Our country's borders tightly closed,
self-isolation through lockdown and masks.
Though the rules all mean to do well,
for us ordinary people
it isn't much better than hell.

This monster is horrid,
it's brought darkness to us all.
It has taken the sunshine away.
Stolen our dignity and smiles.
There are no more hugs or kisses
to show your love and care.
One has to stay away.
It is all so hard to bear.

It has crushed our hope,
caused suffering and pain.
While longing for our loved ones,
both small and big businesses bust,
causing economies to turn to dust.

Fighting this virus has been hard.
So far, the battlefield is littered with death.
There is some success but often fickle,
leaving us all quite scarred.

Dying of COVID-19 is cruel and sad.
One faces their final moments alone
with nobody there to hold their hand
or whisper, 'It's OK to let go.'

Is there any end in sight?
I certainly hope there is.
I believe in the goodness of mankind.
I believe that we will win.

ŠEĆERANA'S CHAMPS-ELYSEES AVENUE

I am sitting on the balcony
in Port Arlington,
looking at the sea.
Today, the water is calm
and so very green.
It takes me back
to fifty years ago,
pre-1971.
To something else green,
not forgotten to me, dear,
but far away, not near.

I am standing on
Kolodvorska road,
on this side of the railway tracks.
Prvomajska street starts
on the other side,
yes, that's something you would find.

In front of me is
the two-way street,
beautiful with
trees lined along each side.
Poplar trees, so very green,
reach up high,
so proud that they
nearly touch the sky.

It is as elegant
as any Parisian attraction
but less famous, of course.
That's why I call it
Šećerana's Champs-Elysees avenue.
Yes, this one may be smaller
but looking at it
gives you great satisfaction.

-1-

Alongside the poplar trees is
a hedgerow,
so nicely clipped,
perhaps by a barber.
very neat, just so.

Down the middle,
neon lights and
a nature strip between
the street and footpaths.
These roads have witnessed much:
happiness, thunder,
broken hearts, tears,
the birth of new loves and such.

This is a residential area.
Kolonija Šećerana's entrance.
The sugar factory's approach
is a picture of excellence
and architectural intelligence.

On the right side, there's
Kristal restaurant,
the park, the library and the cinema.
All gorgeous and romantic.
In one word: fantastic.

The street is tidy and so clean,
kept by Mr Iva Šumanovac's
proud and strict maintenance routine.

Are you still alive Poplars,
my street's slender knights?
Do you still stand on guard,
keeping secrets of hearts breaking
or are your branches now heavy and aching?

-2-

Where are the nature strips?
Did they give way
to a local bar?
Perhaps they're car parks today?

If I were a painter,
these memories
would be a noted painting
in Županja's museum,
upon the main wall, decorating.

It is said
that at the end of life,
everybody returns to the old country,
to one's old place,
back to the lilac tree.

For now, I am back on the balcony
with the sun and
the sea of blue
busy touching the Australian shore,
a place in my heart forevermore.

KOLONIJA ŠEĆERANA WAS, NOW ISN'T

My place of living, growing,
learning and discovering.
Of falling in and out of love,
of shedding tears
always behind your shield.
Breathing that sweet air,
safely together, we healed.

We older generations
know who and what you were.
We know what you had.
You were a unique
hive of young bees.
The mecca of music, dance,
entertainment and sport.
Springboard to many,
one of them me.

To the poor and illiterate
you gave work, food,
dignity, pride, and salvation.
You were the beating heart, a cutie,
Županja's shining beauty.

We had a doctor, a barber,
a baker and a food store.
there was a tiny fruit and veg market
and a butcher shop,
so clean and small,
always kept nice and bright,
just like the butcher Hajlo, I recall.

A hairdresser was a rare treasure,
but we had the best
sugar factory and schools.
Every child whether rich or poor
lived by all the same rules.

-1-

We also had the dentist
who always took at least
one tooth out.
Did he ever save one?
That I doubt.

Kolonija Šećerana was a garden of flowers
full of exquisite scents and colours.
One blossom was mine,
so small, purple and fine.

Many are surprised to find
my childhood and early youth
were so happy.
but to answer why is easy:
it was the time of dreaming,
being, reaching and feeling.

Was it an ideal world?
I didn't know it then.
Youth was the time of
brighter tomorrows
without the responsibilities.
Then, money wasn't all.
One day it had might,
the next, it caused pain and fright.

Now, Kolonija Šećerana
is losing its shine,
but is it by neglect or
from being pushed into decline?

A tornado, we all know its name,
took and blew everything
to the other side,
leaving only pain behind.

-2-

Županja, Mother,
look at your hands.
Do you care equally
for all of your fingers?
I don't know.
One finger is sad and tired,
feeling so very impotent,
yet it knows that it is innocent.

Is life better there now?
I would say yes, for some
who, overnight, so powerful
they have become.

1969 was, to me, an important year.
Županja, you betrayed me
but I have forgiven you.
My excellent marks and education
did not count.
Without powerful kin,
there was no paid job I could get.

Life was difficult
but I packed my pain and pride
into my pocket
and found a path
to a sunburnt country,
a new homeland
where I could live free.

Around the world,
we Šećeranci-Županjci natives
witness this phenomenon,
never forgetting our golden flower
during that period of life,
both theirs and mine,
a time that was great and divine.

Slavonija lives.
Slavonija remembers.
It stores its stories away.
History has a duty
to tell the truth.
History knows.
You can ignore it
but you can never change it.

Kolonija-Šećerana,
you loved and,
in return, were loved.
That love is in our blood.

Kolonija Šećerana,
it is better to be
and lose
than to never be at all.
You were.

-4-

ŽUPANJA RAILWAY STATION

From 1901, she has stood proudly,
performing her duties efficiently.
A most powerful railway empress,
Županja's biggest and greatest
people and goods protectress.

Her heart has beaten tirelessly.
She has received trains
and sent them on their way.
We passengers and goods
welcomed and redirected.
Loved by all, always respected.

Cars were rarities.
Buses were scarce and costly.
Trains were our saviours.
To school and work
they took us
without any fuss.

The station's building was beautiful
in Schoenbrunn style and colours.
A well-known trade mark
of the Austro-Hungarian monarchy,
she stands bravely, always
of her own importance conscious.

In the waiting room stood
a big, black iron furnace.
During cold winter days,
people loved its great hot blaze.

On the left was a lavish garden
full of vegetables and flowers.
It was the stationmaster's wife's
pride and joy.
Everyone always so impressed.

-1-

To the right there was
a small bathroom block
with two squatting toilets.
There was a water tank and
one pull-chain for flushing
but no paper, of course.
One entered the room
without any touching.

Steam locomotives pulled
old trains
leaving clouds of smoke behind.
Some years later,
along came a new, lighter Schienenbus
operated by a diesel engine,
such a gentle, quiet machine.

Hundreds of people
travelled by train,
but when it was time to go home,
the only transport was your feet.
For Šećerana's people, it was easy,
for others, the trip was a little slow.

For four long years,
almost every day,
both morning and at night,
I travelled one way to Vinkovci
and the other back to Županja.
Good morning and see you later.
Good evening and good night.
Back again to the station,
travelling with day's first light.

At the front of the station,
on the corner,
was the jeweller, Iljkić,
a master of his craft.
His door and window
stood behind iron bars,
protecting gems and gold
until they were sold.
On a little further—

-2-

something different
but still quite important—
stood the local pub.
To male travellers and railway men
it was heaven on a cold, rainy day.
Their cooked wine and slivovitz[8]
was prescribed by the doctor
but one, small glass only.
Directions that were followed mostly.

To this golden age
I was a witness,
bystander to Županja station
and all of her greatness.
In '71, time brought change.
Where once numerous trains
had been needed,
by cars, buses and trucks
that need was superseded.

Of this change
I was constantly told
but I have also seen it myself.
Every time I've visited
this once great station,
I've felt so sad,
I've had to be consoled.

Županja station is
much older now
but she is still so beautiful.
Though less noisy,
she is no less honourable,
and always so very memorable.

---

[8] Spirit drink made of plums

ŠEĆERANA'S ACACIAS

Hey, Acacias, hey.
The time has passed.
I don't know when or how.
I have not forgotten you,
even though I am very far away.

Whoever planted you
did well.
a smart deed,
indeed.

You grew into
Šećerana's nameless streets,
a beautiful avenue.
Edged its major pedestrian ways.
What grace.
What a view.

One more tree line
along the wire fence,
loved by the young,
so romantic and divine.

You were glorious
in the month of May.
Green canopies filled with flowers,
thick, white clusters
hanging proudly,
conscious of their magical display.

Most were undecided
as to what was more charming,
what you could see
Or the perfume so intoxicating.

As children, we ate the flowers,
still unopened, young, sweet
and as white as snow,
but that was so very long ago.

You adorned Kolonija Šećerana
and our sweet air you cleaned.
How very useful you were.
Acacias, you simply gleamed.

Are you still living?
Are you still admired
just as you were then?
Are there any dreamers
left now
to smile, to wink at you,
to take a bow?

Hey, Acacias, hey.
Šećerana's beauties.
Its gorgeous,
memorable trees.

WHO IS A SLAVONIAN?

The one born in Slavonia
by a mother,
regardless of her origin.
Slavonia is enriched
with this precious gift.

Whether from Bosnia,
Hercegovina, Dalmatia,
Zagorje, Slavonia,
or any of the rest.
Whether from the north,
south, east or west.

The one who inhaled
Slavonian air with her first breath,
filled her tiny lungs,
then easily exhaled.

The one whose eyes,
small and divine,
opened in Slavonia
for the first time.

The one who took
her first steps there
and spoke her first words,
insecurely
but proudly.

The one kept warm
by the Slavonian sun;
hydrated by Slavonian water;
fed by Slavonian land.

The one who played
in the dust
under a lilac tree.
Who ran barefoot through
meadows, happy and free.

The one fascinated
by that flat land.
Who adored snow and rain
and played in the mud gladly,
loving the earth madly.

The one who admired the
wheat and corn fields, and
fondly spoke
about Slavonian oak.

The one who learnt there
how to read and write.
Who stitched Croatian words
into her soul
just to become whole.

The one who remained
and the one who left sobbing.
Never forgetting
and always longing.

The ones who, after a half-century,
who, 14,092 kilometres away,
carries Slavonia in her heart
with pride every day.

The one who, on the way
to her eternal place,
will fly over Slavonia—
a mother who still waits for
her child to come back and say goodbye,
one more time, with a deep sigh.

The one who, despite having
a happy, new homeland,
still calls Slavonia
her motherland.

That is a Slavonian.

LAPLAND, 2010

After wishing for so long,
we were finally there.
Snow covered, -11°C,
Helsinki, Finland,
on our way to Lapland with
the Aurora Borealis to see,
but there was no guarantee.

The very next day,
we boarded a Tallink & Silja Line ship
to Tallinn, Estonia.
The crossing was choppy and scary.

Tallinn, Estonia's capital city,
was dressed in white snow, -6°C.
Its walled Old Town,
the gothic town hall and more
all looked so regal and pretty.

We took a flight to Ivalo,
very far north,
past the Arctic Circle
to Kakslauttanen Arctic Resort.
Well on our way
on a dark but white -19°C day.

It was dark by 3 pm.
The sunset to return in February
created this wonderland
into a further magical world.

Brilliant, white, squeaking snow
made everything seem brighter.
With twinkling stars above,
cabin and igloo lights below
and streetlights on 24/7,
we were treated to a beautiful show.

-1-

Our choice of accommodation
for the very first night
was a heated, frost-free glass igloo
where we hoped to see
the elusive northern lights.

Waiting, watching the cloudy sky
from my comfy bed with the
door open in a room too hot,
green and reddish light dancing
around the moon was all I got.

Husky dog sledding
through the snow-covered silent forest
and over the frozen river
left us mesmerised
and by -30°C, we hugged and kissed.

Deep in the forest,
in a wooden tepee,
we had a hot lunch,
an authentic Sami dish
made of cheese, carrots, peas and fish.

Later, a snowmobile safari
from Saariselkä Village
up to Kaunispää Fell,
close to the Russian border,
still hoping to experience
the northern lights' spell.

Temperature: -30°C. Our camera froze
with no aurora borealis in sight.
As we turned our snowmobile,
I looked back one more time.
Bingo! White-grey curtain-like lights
just for me. It was so real.

-2-

Log cabins and furniture
masterfully handcrafted
from rare standing dead pines,
the kelo trees:
national pure gold;
a true sight to behold.

Walking through the pristine snow,
snowflakes falling and dancing.
Mimi sledded downhill
as excited as a child.
A sight to remember,
a sight so entrancing.

This holiday was fascinating.
The snow-covered country was enchanting.
Our activities were exhilarating.

One minus that I must give them:
the resort owners and staff
spoke little to no English,
so communication was tough,
understanding was rough.

I imagined Sami people would
do their country proud.
I knew they could.
They knew they should.

SNOWY ŽUPANJA

Please be generous.
Give me a white Christmas
and a snowy New Year.
Make this visit a happy one,
my old place, my dear.

This was my request
to you, Županja,
before my visit 2010-2011.
My first winter visit
in thirty-nine years.
I dreamt.
I hoped.

We arrived on Christmas Eve,
happy to see all.
Family, friends,
and this dear place,
still not dressed in white
like it was in the past
when I saw it last.

Christmas Eve and Day
came and went
beautifully, with dignity,
but without snow, still a little sad.

Boxing Day came
with surprising joy.
Perfect snowflakes fell,
dancing elegantly,
creating fine, white lace
to dress my old place.

-1-

Snowflakes and we people
are similar.
Each snowflake, like
each person, is unique.
There are never
two truly identical, never, ever.

Hotel Jelen,
through your window
I saw the clear, silent night.
I watched the twinkling stars
in all their special might.

Multi-coloured Christmas lights
adorned the buildings and trees.
Fabulous illumination.
Very impressive decoration.

A white Christmas
and snowy New Year
were my dream.
A different world,
clean, tender, innocent.
A gift given to earth,
making one happy and content.

Covered in snow, Museum Čardak
stood at ease like a border guard
protecting Županja's history.
To pass the time,
it counted and observed
each snowflake's design.

The Sava river and its embankment
stood in a firm, snowy embrace.
I don't know if was
due to the cold
or just mutual admiration.
Either way, it was a
beautiful association.

Kolonija Šećerana looked
like a fairy tale;
its trees crowned with snowy pearls.
Houses, lanes, streets,
restaurant and the park
formed a dear picture,
youthful and white.
Šećerana's pride. Šećerana's delight.

New Year's Eve was different.
At dances long ago,
the square filled with happy people,
with music, dance and song.
It was no longer the same but still nice.
Lots of memories.
Fireworks sent the old year away
and welcomed the new day.

Walking on the snow,
hearing the squeak.
Snowflakes falling, dancing.
Feeling fresh, cold air on my face.
A scene and experience
to remember. a winter haven
for this content Croatian.

This visit was touching.
Županja was hospitable
and my experience was exciting.

Županja, thank you.
You gave me
a white Christmas and New Year.
You made this visit
a happy one.
You were caring.
You were giving.
You were snowy.

-3-

IT WAS LIKE THIS. IT STILL IS

i. It was like this.

From early childhood,
I had a dream
of becoming a nurse,
of looking after people
when they were unwell and feeble.

The school for nurses in Vinkovci[9]
did not accept me.
My school results were excellent,
but even with a top score,
there was no guarantee.

My score was 100%, but
when you are a poor child,
you are already aware
that you don't count.
Without money, no one cares.

I put my disappointment aside
and enrolled in high school.
With the scouts and girl guides
I went away camping,
hoping my pain would subside.

Without my knowledge,
a good, powerful man named
Rade Pavlović[10] heard of the injustice.
He didn't approve.
He enrolled me in nursing school
and gave me a scholarship.
I was happy to take
this long-desired study trip.

-1-

---

9   Town in Croatia
10   CEO of the town's sugar factory

I found him
forty-three years later,
to thank him and to ask,
'Why did you help this
poor Croatian child?'
He answered,
'It was the right thing to do.
I could, and I wanted to.
I was once in the same
predicament, too.'

In my first year at school,
there were four classes.
By Christmas, one had disappeared.
By the end of the school year,
one more class was cleared.

Time moved fast
in happiness and hard work.
With the final exam
perfectly passed,
I become a good nurse at last.

Županja's Health Centre
had no job for me,
but they convinced me
to volunteer first.
I agreed regretfully.

It took eleven months
for my eyes to open to possibility.
I grew wings one day
and decided to fly away.

Australia welcomed me
and restored my belief
in integrity and a fair go.
It gave me back my
self-respect and pride,
all that I lost so long ago.

-2-

ii. It still is.

Hotel Dubrovnik, Zagreb, 2010,
I sat, enjoying a short black.
Near my table
were two couples.
The older man said to the younger,
'Excellent, you got the job!
Who fixed it for you?
Who did you go through?'

Anger and darkness came over me.
This world was still the same.
Again, someone better
but minus the connection
did not get the job.
Corruption equals selection.

Sorrow enveloped me.
A sad tear slid down my face
for the lost half of a century,
for the unrealised dreams,
for the wilted flowers of justice,
for a country's accepted disgrace.

In the past,
all wrongs were blamed
on the system of communism,
and rightfully so.
But please explain
what is happening now.
Does anybody really know?

Vinkovci and Županja
did not want me.
Australia opened its doors.
Through hard work, respect and loyalty,
I returned the favour joyously.

-3-

Why do many think
we immigrants suffer here,
that we don't belong?
Let me tell you,
the air that I breathe,
the sun that keeps me warm,
the water that I drink,
the land that feeds me,
it is all mine.
This is my new home country
that has made me happy and free.

Nothing will ever
erase the love
for my old place,
my childhood homeland.
Never.

Like the servant Yerney[11],
I continue my search for justice.
In my head and soul,
through the thick fog
that chokes equality like a wild hog.

It will get there!
It has to.
Obviously not tomorrow,
but it will arrive in the arms
of the rising sun
one morning,
when it's all clean and done.

It was like this.
It still is.

-4-

---

11   A character in a book by Ivan Cankar

LILY IN ŽUPANJA

I had a wish.
It came true.
Lily in Županja,
cradle of my childhood,
my early youth.
A history woven long ago,
now hers to get to know.

Lily, our first grandchild,
little Australian
here to feel, to see
the places where it all began,
the birth of her own clan.

There was so much for her
to experience and see:
the beautiful town hall
in famous Schönbrunn colours,
and the old church
where Baka and Dida
got married twice,
as per that time's law.

On the same river embankment
that I had, she strolled.
By the same winding river,
with the crane's silhouette
in the distance,
she was charmed.
So much to behold.

She visited the same beach
from my youth,
stepped on the muddy ground
where a shiny river shell she found.

We toured Kolonija Šećerana.
Small streets, shut shops,
the cinema and library's ghosts.
The dry, neglected fountain
minus the brass frogs,
now destroyed by wild hogs.

Looking at her
as she stood
in the ruins of my school,
I was melancholic,
remembering myself
as a nine-year-old,
proud, happy and bold.

She could not understand
why window shutters
were broken.
Windows wide open
in heavy rain,
the walls damp, decayed
and in such a sad state.
This wasn't the
apartment of my stories,
Kolonija 18,
once so special and great.

In the once summer garden
of the Kristal restaurant,
we had drinks.
This or that,
coffee and the rest.
Lily had Cockta,
full of bubbles,
the best.

-2-

Everything different,
yet everything still the same.
Poplar trees and grass, the same green.
The air still gentle
but the hedges were long gone.
I even heard the
Kristal band play
but only in my memories
of a time very far away.

We went into the dance hall,
up to the balcony,
down the winding stairs
to the dance floor.
The sound of a waltz played
only in my ear.
We danced a few steps,
nice and slow
like I did so very long ago.

We took her to the
beautiful railway station,
once the transportation empress,
but nowadays, almost helpless.

Lily survived on pastries
and some doughnuts
bought each morning
By Milenko,
nice, fresh and hot.
He was an angel,
so, for this, I say,
thanks a lot.

-3-

Lily ate a chevap or two
at Café Lambada.
There was also pita bread
but ice cream was number one,
she definitely preferred that instead.
On every visit, they knew
her favourite flavour,
so to her pure bliss,
they always had it ready,
waiting for our little miss.

This was a new world
for our Lily.
Not too strange
but different, yes.
A world that was still hers,
nonetheless.
Our little Aussie,
for just a short while,
was a happy little Županjka
with a big, sweet smile.

THE EXODUS FROM ŽUPANJA

Long ago,
at the end of the sixties,
my then-boyfriend had a wish
to live in Australia,
with freedom of thought
and success to accomplish.

He asked me,
'Would you wish the same?
Would you ever?'
'What? Australia? So far away.
No, not me. No, never.'

To realise his dream,
to work, create and be free,
he had to leave the old country,
to disappear, to flee.

To go with him,
leave my friends and family,
my streets and trees,
my beloved Županja,
I begged, 'Do not ask me, please.'

He kept quiet.
He was wise.
After our wedding,
I opened my eyes.
My decision was revised.

When I saw reality,
I felt great sadness.
Županja had betrayed me.
The decision was made,
so for Australia we left.
Despite a better life to find,
I went sobbing and bereft.

-1-

In the late sixties, early seventies,
Županja was a poignant picture.
People saying their goodbyes,
full of tears and muffled sighs.

Exactly how many left Županja,
I am really not sure.
What were their reasons?
Poverty, injustice, politics,
we just could no longer endure.

It was said
that we immigrants
were mostly uneducated,
from villages,
but not quite.

The truth is, it was a
persistent, oppressive,
steel-booted, suffocating brute
that pushed us to emigration.
Where we had only had
helplessness and discrimination,
Australia kindly offered immigration.

We didn't lack
intelligence, courage or goodwill.
All of these qualities blossomed
under Australia's just sun.
Here, all are respected,
here, all are welcome.

Emigration was a chain process.
One emigrated family
pulled another.
The numbers grew.
Big changes were made
for our children and for us.
For a nicer future,
it was a small price to be paid.

Ah, there was longing.
Tears were often shed.
In time, we replaced
those tears with smiles instead.

Many of us
still live in Melbourne.
We are happy to meet
and see each other.
We all have one thing in common:
our love for our old place,
Županja, in this case.

We achieved success.
We earned our educations.
All secured through hard work
and knowledge,
not by political or nepotic patronage.

Is Županja happier without us?
This I do not know.
Perhaps Županja does not care.
One thing I do know is,
even though I found a place,
a home that is honest, just and fair,

you can remove the girl from Županja,
but you cannot remove Županja from the girl.

ŽUPANJA'S IMMIGRANTS IN MELBOURNE

We are here.
We arrived a half-century ago,
full of hope
for a brighter tomorrow
but with heavy hearts
and hidden sorrow.

We left our old home,
our birthplace,
in search of a land
that would understand
and give us a helping hand.

We travelled differently.
Some by air, speedily,
hugged by clouds, dreamily.
Many came by ocean,
getting seasick
from the ship's motion.

We worked hard and earned.
We spent and saved wisely.
With prosperity achieved,
our desired respect was received.

What about our children?
It was up to them.
Many got an education,
university degrees completed,
some two or even three.
Some trained in craft and trade.
Those who did not want school,
prospered in other ways.

We meet on occasion,
for dinner and dances and else.
For celebrations of the New Year,
at concerts of Croatian singers,
oldies from our times.
Our events are always happy,
in our hearts we hold them dear.

Do we regret coming here?
No.
We found a new home.
Melbourne received us
and, with its embrace, shielded us.
We were given the opportunity
to make our new Australian identity.

We are content and
we are happy,
but a small spark
for our old place
flickers in our hearts,
never losing its shine.
A flicker that holds,
eternal and divine.

SLAVONIAN NIGHTINGALE

He flew away
into the arms of
the rising sun,
from his old place
to a new
everlasting embrace.

Did he fly over
his old nest in Osijek[12],
his birth town?
Osijek awaited him.
With the sound of
he left with the scent
of the morning,
he was sent on his way
to his eternal stay.

Though other nightingales
will return after winter,
it is not so for this one.
We all know his name:
Krunoslav 'Kićo' Slabinac[13].
Our proud Slavonian.
Our nightingale he became.

Next spring, when
other nightingales
start singing,
one special voice,
Kićo's magic voice,
will be missing.

A voice can't be bought,
stolen, acquired or learnt.
With it, one is born.
With it, one lives.
With it, one dies.

---

12   Town in Croatia
13   Name of a Croatian pop singer

Kićo's song is medicine
for a broken heart,
for sadness and for darkness.
He is the best always
in so many different ways.

His Slavonian folk songs
still touch my soul.
They make me jump and dance.
Ignoring my weary knee,
I forget about poor old me.

Be they folk or other kinds,
they are loved equally,
Kićo's songs, definitely.

His visits to Australia,
every time, were better
for our sentimentality
than any psychotherapy.

His farewell concert,
October 2019,
was emotional.
His career's 50th anniversary,
simply sensational.

For our nightingale,
I have only three little words:
Kićo, thank you!

We lost
what the angels won.

-2-

PRESERVE THE CROATIAN WORD

Every time I have visited
since the Croatian Homeland War,
they have corrected my spoken Croatian,
never conscious of their deviation.
Listen, enough!
With all due respect,
your spoken Croatian is imperfect.

I watch Croatian Dnevnik every day.
Grief overwhelms me.
Journalists, politicians, public communicators,
educated people and ordinary men
have allowed English words
to sneak into their speaking.
Why? Is it to show off?
What are they seeking?

When I asked the reason,
they answered, 'Technology. The internet.'
That is only an excuse.
It will make the Croatian language sick
with its unnecessary use.

Language is alive.
It keeps changing.
That is normal,
but change should excel
the Croatian word.
That would be preferred.

We criticised Hungarianisation
and, of course, Serbian hybridisation,
but with right, as they were imposed.
What about the Anglicisation
that you so willingly use?
I'd call that self-barbarisation.
Your use of modern words
doesn't make you bigger,
better or more intelligent.
It makes you poorer.

I've lived in Australia
for the last fifty years,
speaking two languages every day,
each chosen by need.
These languages have not become
Croatian-English or English-Croatian.
They are still one or the other,
indeed.

Tell me, why are
many languages preserved?
From the beginning
until now, they have not dissolved
into a single global language,
they have not evolved.

The Croatian language is irreplaceable.
Preserve it. It is a giant.
Build a linguistic raft.
Let Croatian outlast
this English blast.

Croatians, teach your children
to protect the Croatian word,
to resist modern influence
and to be strong,
not to simply go along.
Only a Croat can
teach a Croat child
how to learn the Croatian language
with heart, soul and mind.

If language is lost,
you lose your identity,
you lose your ethnicity.

Where do you find
the most exquisite words?
Not elsewhere, not yonder.
You already have them.

The Croatian word is pure wonder.
The Croatian word is
a linguistic pearl.
Our word is precious.
Our word is sterling.
Our word is worth preserving.

MY MAMA

Now, in the winter of my life,
memories flood back
about Mama, both
my sisters' and mine,
from a hard but dear time.

Born at the start
of the twentieth century
in Kopanice, Bosnia,
a long way away,
on one spring day.

Formal schooling: zero.
Official status: illiterate.
Life knowledge: rich.
Far ahead of her generation,
life was her education.

After the war, life was tough
for Šokci in Bošnjaci.
She worked in a field all day,
paid with a kilo of flour.
Such was their power.

1955 was her lucky year.
She got a job
in Županja's sugar factory.
She cleaned the bathrooms
with pride, happily
and efficiently.

She had six children.
She lost two sons.
Four daughters survived.
Our father was horrid.
He felt deprived.

-1-

Mama raised us four.
She worked so hard.
Though earned money
was the minimum,
she stretched it
to the maximum.

She taught us that
kindness, honesty, loyalty,
respect and hard work
are values
more important than money
in her view.

Even at times of scolding,
she never used an ugly word.
I was never smacked.
She was just like that.
Always very gentle, in fact.

On cold winter days,
Mama gave us kids
piggyback rides
from the bathroom to the kitchen,
the only warm room in the house.
To me, it was always so fun.
To me, her rides were grouse.

As a child, I always wondered
how she managed to create
beautiful meals from so little.
Now, as an adult, I know,
it was Mama's magic
that made it so.

Eventually, life changed.
To Australia we immigrated.
Our love for Mama
was more than reciprocated.

Mama loved and spoiled our children.
For breakfast, she made them pancakes.
She played the card game Sevens with them
and always had an extra seven.
She was the best baka.
I wonder if she's still cheating
now in heaven.

I miss her smile,
her brown eyes,
her warm hugs, her quick step
and her light touch.
I'll always love her so very much.

If only I could again have
her damper or crumpled pastry,
her cornbread, her polenta,
or her burek with or without cheese,
I would think it came
from heaven above,
sent by Mama with love.

Mama is there now, I know.
As she was leaving,
she looked at all of us,
called us her doves,
took one last breath
and left without fuss.

This was my Mama.

-3-

POOR CHILD'S IRRELEVANCE

It was reality.
It is and will always be.
From the beginning
until the end of time,
it is life's design.

It's known by all.
There are many causes.
One thing is to know about it,
another
to live it,
to carry that burden,
to live that life
carved by an unfair knife.

When you are that child,
you don't understand how
but you feel, you know.
Somehow, you are easily recognised.

Superficial things are visible.
Your school bag is old.
Your books are preloved.
Your pencils are sharpened by knife, roughly,
not with a pencil sharpener, perfectly.

Your clothes are clean but hand-me-downs
and your school sleepers aren't from a shop.
They are different,
made at home by mum.
Nice but not the same,
I mean.

Some children will always find
someone else to play with
in the school ground,
someone of their own kind.

-1-

Invisible things
are more important.
How many books
has that child read?
How fast does that child memorise?
How easily are geography and history learnt?
How quickly are mathematical problems solved?

How does that child feel?
How big is her pain?
How desperate is her hope
that these times won't last,
that they will
firmly stay in her past?

The tragedy is even greater
when the teacher is indifferent,
never giving the deserved mark
to a child who is poor and irrelevant.

What is this child's future?
Not bright.
Only a miracle could
see her future secured.

No child is unimportant.
Food, water, the sun and love
are needed by all,
but more so by a child,
innocent, weak and small.

Should the child pay
for its parents' sins?
No. Look more carefully.
I am me,
the bearer of my being,
don't you see?

Support and belief,
a single open door,
that is all that's needed
for the irrelevant
to become relevant.

MY WINTER

Not willingly
but naturally,
I entered this time
of my life,
occasionally limping
but still great, still fine.

The train of life
rushed without stopping
through innocent spring,
hot exciting summer,
or kind autumn.
It entered secretive winter,
at times coughing, hopping.

I didn't buy a ticket
for this destination,
but when you are 70 years old,
you get it as a gift.
This I was never told.

My autumn was giving,
long and warm.
Perhaps it did not rush
towards the cold winter,
but that time has gone;
a new part of life has been born.

My winter has arrived,
gentle for now,
without icicles and snow.
I'm not kidding.
Its power is huge,
I know.

-1-

A worse cold will come,
slowing down my steps,
wrinkling my skin,
playing with my memory.
It's an awful possibility.
To stop it isn't in my ability.

My joints and bones
are great for now.
They lost the battle.
They are afraid
of doctor's blades.

Hot flushes have gone.
They are only a memory.
I wish them a nice trip.
Don't come back;
you will not find me.
I have won.

My headaches also retreated.
Those painful days have
stopped with time,
totally defeated.

My body is changing.
Not with my blessing.
COVID-19 kilos have moved in
with a sly grin.

-?-

There are intraocular lenses
in my eyes now.
Cataracts ruined my sight,
that ugly, brutal blight.

One thing is still surprising—
my mind is clear.
It's eager to work,
creating in third gear
but aware that time is short,
it would appear.

Write it all down,
describe everything,
edit it all,
so that the memories
of my life's
long, rich drive
are not lost.

Through the window
of this winter,
I can see the sunshine.
This is my Indian summer.
My winter will be a stunner.

TUC-TUC[14]

This time of year
wakes up memories
of times long gone,
when money was a rarity
but the small things,
both given and received,
meant sincerity.

Like my mama then,
I collect onion peel,
every year
in Australia, here.

To keep our traditions
—important for this day—
I colour Easter eggs
and get unusual hues,
every time,
something totally new.

What is this colour's name?
It's not brown.
I really don't know.
It is special.
I find myself in a dilemma,
so I simply call it Lukena.

Purchased egg colours
are never as nice.
This one is wonderful.
It is natural and clean.
Its beauty needs to be seen.

-1-

---

14   Slang for *tucanje jaja*, a traditional Easter egg cracking game.

Eggs used to be sold by the piece
not in a carton.
As a dozen or more
was difficult before.

Eggs were respected
and by children, they were
very much enjoyed,
especially when boiled.

A half-century ago,
tuc-tuc,
the game of
cracking Easter eggs,
had rules.
It could bring happiness or despair.
It was your game to win or lose.

The egg with
both sides cracked lost.
That was a fact.
The winner went home happy
with more eggs as
evidence of his or her skill
and the strength of his or her will.

Here in Australia,
tradition is fading.
People think new is better.
They fall in love with the new,
history doesn't matter.

In Australia,
the Easter Bunny
brings chocolate eggs,
sweet, not real,
with much more appeal.

A real egg's worth was
great in the past.
Now it's lost.
Today, by chocolate,
aside it's been tossed.

With chocolate eggs,
there is no tuc-tuc.
They would break.
There is no winner.
There is no loser.

The word pisanica[15]
and so many more
are new and strange to me.
I have to consult Google
for information on
this new word's definition.

Dudek[16] said once,
'Language: Croatians use
but don't understand.'

Colouring Easter eggs
with an onion peel and
cracking them
is an old custom,
a tradition.
May it be forever observed
and for the future preserved.

So, I colour
Easter eggs each year.
At our Easter picnics,
we play tuc-tuc.
We have a winner.
We have a loser.

-3-

---

15   A decorated Croatian Easter egg
16   Old Croatian comedian

TOO LATE

It's a grey and rainy day.
Same as it was then,
thirty years ago.
There is no sunshine
to lighten the thoughts of
sad, regretful me.
No sunshine
to warm my memory.

There is so much
I would like to know
and to tell you,
but time will not
turn back. It cannot.

I should have
given you more time,
learnt and discovered
the little things in your past.
It is too late now.
I accept this. I must.

Why didn't I give you time?
I do not know.
Why do we take
each other for granted?
Why do we leave questions
and words for tomorrow?

Will tomorrow come?
It is never certain.
That's why we must ask and say
while there is time today.

You are not here anymore
but the words and questions are.
Words still unspoken,
questions still unasked.

The questions are forever silent
with answers that are sealed.
The words that I left for tomorrow
will forever be concealed.

-2-

THE MAGIC OF LIFE

It is invisible, intangible,
powerful and irresistible.
It is needed for happiness.
It is ageless.

Agitated tense thoughts heal.
It frightens tornadoes away.
It brings the sea breeze.
A tired body to appease.

It warms you when cold.
It makes you cry when you're sad.
It is more precious than gold.

It enters your body and soul
and lifts you up onto
the wings of a flamingo.
It takes you into the magic
of a folk dance, waltz or tango.

It encourages love.
It refreshes memories
of unfulfilled promises.
It heals pain
again and again.

It's different, like us.
Not the same.
What is this force?
Music. Music is its name.

Life without music
would be like
black coffee with no sugar,
flowers with no scent,
food with no salt.
It would be the world
without colour,
books with no letters.

Music is the composition of
light, clean air,
food, water and love.
Music is life's supreme contribution.
Music is nature's perfect creation.

FREEZING AGONY

I am cold,
so very cold.
Is there any
tiny bit of warmth
for me to grab and hold?

Blanket. Doona. Blanket.
There's a mountain on top of me.
Still, there's no use,
a crisis is coming,
that I can definitely see.

I am freezing.
I am shaking.
My teeth are chattering, too.
I am thinking, *oh goodness,
what am I to do?*

A beautiful hot shower,
such short relief it gave.
Five minutes of calm
before this dark offensive
grew more horrid and intensive.

Cold as a tsunami rising,
preparing for release.
I beg and plead this nausea to stop.
Just give me back some peace.

I am turning into a block of ice.
Such cold is misery.
Free me from this churning pain,
please take me from this agony.

ALONE

Into this life,
you arrive alone.
From that same life,
you depart alone.

Your whole life, people
buzz around you.
To you, some are known
but most are not.
They are there
by chance
at that very spot.

It gives you the perception
that you are not on your own.
Perhaps physically, yes,
but it really is
a major deception.

When you shut your eyes,
hoping to go to sleep,
you are you,
only one, not two.

You might find yourself
standing in a fog,
confused, lost,
and in much pain,
asking, 'Where to?
Left or right?
Is there any hope in sight?'

You might think
the dark is attractive,
but, hey, look there!
There are rays of sunshine,
light and warmth
if you turn the other way.
The light whispers,
'Please, come to us,
we pray.'

ŠEĆERANA'S CHRISTMAS, MINE, ONCE UPON A TIME

There was once
an urban housing estate
where the word Christmas
wasn't spoken loudly,
although we wished we could
shout it proudly.

There were many of us,
from all sides;
north, south,
east and west,
all the colours,
like a beautiful rainbow,
the best.

We didn't speak publicly
about Christmas.
We kept it quiet.
We knew it was safer
politically.

If you had faith,
celebrated Christmas,
attended a church,
you were thought *backwards*.
Such an ugly word.

If your family were
Bosnian-Croatian,
some thought
you could not be bright,
but, of course,
we knew they weren't right.

At times, Mama went to church.
We children went rarely,
one might say barely.
Faith was personal.
In our family, it was

-1-

nursed and kept
by Mama
with the deepest respect.

Christmas Eve came.
Happy and loud,
we decorated our tree
with shiny wrapped lollies
and crepe paper ribbons.
That was all we had,
but with our efforts
we were so glad.

During the night,
Mama brought in some straw.
She placed it
in the corner of the kitchen,
threw in some wrapped lollies,
walnuts and coins.

Christmas morning,
we children sprinted to the straw.
With playful squeaks,
we successfully explored.

For breakfast:
warm bread, bacon,
eggs, sausages and aspic,
a beautiful Christmas classic.

On the table, in the centre,
a candle and Christmas wheat.
The wheat was green,
healthy and young.
With it, the table was complete.

Saint Catherine was
extra kind at times.
Just before Christmas
she would bring snow
like a gift to us children,
only hers to bestow.

Creating snow angels,
snowballing,
running through the white,
admiring the snowflakes,
it was free for all.
A joy for us,
both big and small.

Not everyone had a sled.
If you didn't,
you enjoyed the view
and watched instead.

Christmas lunch
was something else.
Fine food, nice treats.
All sorts of beauties
consumed with ease.

Gifts bought from shops
we really didn't get.
We knew it wasn't possible,
so our expectations were met.

Hoping for store-bought gifts
would have been like wishing
to fly to the moon,
or to wear velvet and silk,
or to drink bird milk.
It was not possible, never.
One would have waited forever.

Santa Claus existed,
but he was always late.
For Christmas he never came
which was always such a shame.

Despite what I didn't have,
my childhood memories
are precious.
They are my mama's creations,
priceless and ageless.

If only my grandkids knew
what kind of Christmases I had.
All humble.
All significant.
All unforgettable.

I wish you
a merry Christmas,
lots of health,
warmth, peace, light
and inner wealth.

MEMORIES

Memories, memories,
take me there
on the wings of notes,
with a gentle breeze,
across the oceans and rivers,
over the mountains and lakes
to my old place,
to a time I wish to retrace.

There, where I left
my first steps
of tango and waltz.
There, where there are
old oak forests,
fields of corn,
sunflowers and wheat.
There, where even muddy
sugar beet is dear and sweet.

I wish to smell
wild strawberries
and the sweet air
of sugar production.
I wish to feel the breath
of my childhood and early youth,
of my past innocent delight,
so light, so very bright.

I want to say
to my old place,
'I forgive you
for all the pain and sorrow.
I am happy now.
I want you to know.'

Tomorrow, take me closer,
not very far,
to where my new home is,
where my achievements are.

Take me to the time
when I became Mother and
brought children
into the world.
Take me to when I
welcomed my grandchildren.
These times are pure gold.

Take me through the
many years of my work.
Let me feel the joy felt
each time I helped
relieve the pain,
bringing comfort to the sick
again and again.

There is so much
in a long life:
marriage, family,
friends, travelling,
happiness, sadness, hurt.
All mine to recollect,
to analyse
and, from oblivion, to protect.

Often, memories come
unannounced.
At times I don't know
how or why.
Often they come
the same way
each day.

Will they find their way?
I am so far away.
Many years have passed.
Life has moved on.
Can the clock turn back?
It cannot.
It will not.

Memories are food
for the body and soul.
Without them,
we are hollow shells,
empty and washed out,
without a doubt.

Life, I beg you,
don't steal my memories.
Without them,
life isn't worth living.
Without my memories,
to live I am unwilling.

MULWALA LAKE

An eerie and strange
but not frightening sight.
Lake Mulwala.
Majestic ghostly
river red gums
stand proudly in the water,
holding their posts,
attracting Murray cod
and other fish.
On the shore,
a fisherman patiently waits,
holding his fishing rod.

The sunrise is a picture to see.
Dark grey at the top,
then bright orange
changing into yellow
meeting the dark green
treetops across the lake.
The water, smooth and calm,
reflects the tint of sunrise.
Blue breaks through,
giving the water unbelievable charm.

Each day is so warm,
in the sun, hotter still,
but the deep tree shade
and refreshing cool breeze
makes it all comfortable
with ease.

Numerous seagulls
and noisy cockatoos
inhabit the trees.
Cockatoos are forever screeching,
their high, deafening
notes reaching.

-1-

There is a resident drake
in our holiday park,
as white as snow
with a bright yellow beak
and a sweet, curled tail.
It waddles to our cabins
every evening,
charming us
for dinner without fail.

Water has this power,
whether calm or restless.
It says,
'Look at me.
I am mighty.
I am giving
but not forgiving.
Without me,
there is no living.'
The Murray River
is our empress.
She is
this region's protectress.

ŽUPANJA'S HOT, HUMID SUMMERS, MINE, ONCE UPON A TIME

I am sitting
on the balcony,
having a cup of tea.
What is that, over there?
Graceful black swans
gliding on the beach,
of their beauty
they are unaware.

Today the sea is greyish-blue
like the sky.
Bonaca[17]. Totally calm.
Smooth like glass.
It sparkles and shines like brass.

There isn't any breeze.
All is resting.
All is dreaming.

It's already so hot that
even the birds are hiding.
Not one is tweeting.

The humidity
takes me back
to a time long gone,
to Županja's hot,
humid summers.
Memories of a Županja's child,
after sixty years survived.

Early in the mornings,
while it was still cool,
we shooed flies
out of the apartment.
Our windows

---

17   Croatian for a calm sea

didn't have flyscreens.
We shut the windows
and the shutters too,
blissful, made of timber.
We didn't have air conditioning
and there was definitely
no swimming pool
to keep us nice and cool.

People of my class
didn't have fridges.
We only saw ice
during the snowy winter.
Juices and fizzy drinks
were unknown.
Perhaps unusual, you might think.

Water was our salvation,
not bought
but from the tap.
For us, of course,
the healthiest
and best.

Homemade ice cream,
lemonade and orange drink
could be bought in a little shop
if you had the money,
but we didn't have any,
we didn't have a penny.

There was only one
simple ice cream shop
in Županja's centre,
but it was so far away
in the mind
of a poor Šećerana child.

It wasn't clear to me
how they made
lemonade and orangeade.
There were no
lemons or oranges
in Županja then!
I suppose it was a
trick of the trade.

People who had wells
cooled watermelons
and all sorts of things in them.
Us Šećeranci did not.
Our building's walls
were thick and solid,
keeping our apartment,
especially the pantry,
so nice and cold.

When I was older,
if Mama let me,
I would go to the Sava river
for a swim
to feel fresher and colder.

The trees provided shade,
mostly enough.
When one is young and healthy,
nature comes to your aid.

The heat and humidity
didn't bother the young much.
It was easy.
Youth is strong and such
Those days were loved
and are still remembered.

-3-

Now, life has changed.
Air conditioning is
in most houses and cars.
There are drinks of all kinds,
whether cold or not,
for one to find.

Ice cream is kept at home
in a deep freezer.
It is taken for granted,
not desired like before.
No, not anymore.

This last period
of my life
is an interesting harbour.
It's full of strength, contentment
and inner wealth.

Away from my memories,
I am back on the balcony.
The sea, still a greyish-blue,
caresses the Australian shore.
Oh, Summer. What a view.

-4-

BOSNIANS ARE PEOPLE

An acquaintance told me
an awful story
the other day,
one that is true,
and for me, painful,
I might say.

About fifty years ago,
she married, happily,
a young man from a
Slavonian village near Županja.
He was from a Šokci family.

She was invited
by her sister-in-law
to go to the shop
in the village centre
and was delighted.

There she saw a group
standing, waiting.
She asked her sister-in-law,
'Who are those people?'
The answer:
'They are not people.
They are Bosnians.'

Hearing my friend's story,
I saw black.
My head was about to crack.

This took me back
to the fifties and sixties.
A time of great poverty
in general
but especially for Bosnians
on the other side
of the river Sava.
Poverty made them
available for hire,
a cheap commodity.

They came in groups;
Bosnian men and women
with their own hoes
and other agricultural tools.
Those were the rules.

They were on display
like at a trade show,
waiting to be hired
by local landowners
as required.

I used to see them
on the train.
Other travellers
glanced at them only,
not wanting to witness
this harsh reality.

Times changed.
Germany opened its doors,
giving Bosnians an opportunity
to eliminate poverty
and find their deserved dignity.

Bosnians on the
other side of the river Sava
are people.
They always have been,
and they always will be.

They used to be poor.
They have always worked hard.
They are worthy of respect.
They are proud, they are fine.
They are, and always will be, mine.

CLOSE YOUR EYES

My eyes are closed.
I am standing
in our front garden.
I can see the number 18.

A light spring breeze
is caressing my face
with love and grace.

A strong lilac fragrance
comes to me
from the purple flowers
on an old,
proud lilac tree.

I turn my head
to the left.
The breeze brings
the sweet scent
of an early Petrovka apple tree
from fresh blossoms,
pink-white and awesome.

We climb the tree
like squirrels,
conquering high branches,
taking our chances.

Shhh. Shhh.
The chirping of swallows,
those small black and white beauties,
sounds so very clear,
right near here.

They have returned
to their old nest,
their known place,
to us, in this case.

-1-

I crouch
to get the hyacinth's scent,
here, very much present.

A little to the right
are snowdrops.
Shy, innocent, white.
They are the picture
of purity and delight.

Next to them
are small violets
with a scent soft and elusive,
to other scents, occlusive.

I move forward
to open the small front gate.
What have I touched?
It is a hedge, a fence
to all of Šećerana's streets,
both narrow and wide,
along each side.

Two more steps.
I am standing on the street.
Krc. Krc.
I know.
This is *šljaka*[18]
well-levelled by feet.

Its feel is very familiar
to my knees.
They remember
šljaka well
from the scraped skin
every time I fell.

---

18 Reprocessed, granulated SLAG, used to cover unsealed streets and roads

Stop.
Wait.
Where are you going?
Come back!

Such a familiar voice.
A beautiful sound
that forces me to
turn around.

Through my closed eyes,
I see Mama
at the upper window,
young, beaming,
absolutely gleaming.

I squeeze my eyes tightly
so I can watch her longer.
This moment
is very potent.

This sight is enchanting.
My mum's dear face,
at this time,
in this place, captivating.

R

R is the twenty-third letter
of the Croatian alphabet.

Is it problematic?
Not for many.
To me, it stood
as an annoying thorn
in the side of my childhood.

Many loved
children's games like
ring-a-ring-a-rosies,
or competitions in fast pronouncing.
R R R R R.
Br Br Br Br Br.
Words like rat, run, rug, rock,
all start with R.
This was big trouble for me.
It was obvious
for everyone to see.

Though the letter R is pretty,
for some kids, it is very tricky.
It has to be pronounced,
as per orthography,
correct and clear
for all to hear.

When I was little,
I couldn't pronounce *R*.
I wasn't able to.
I didn't have a clue.

So *R R R R R*
became *L L L L L.*
Br Br Br Br Br
became *Bl Bl Bl Bl Bl.*
Ring-a-ring-a-rosies
became *ling-a-ling-a-losies.*
Words like rat, run and rock
became lat, lun and lock.

Problem number one
was my name: Ruža.
When asked,
'What is your name?'
My answer was *Luža*.

My friends
didn't tease me.
They considered me funny,
a very little honey bunny.

I was never
taken to the doctor.
I was not unwell.
One could tell.

Logopaedics did not exist.
The belief was
this problem
would come good
sooner or later
on its own.
It was well known.

With time
and hard work,
ling-a-ling-a-losies
became *ring-a-ring-a-rosies*.

And just in time,
right before I started school
with my teacher:
Radojka.

Glossary

Baka: Croatian word for grandmother.

Boris Kidrič: the name of the primary school I attended.

Dida: Croatian word for grandfather.

Kolonija Šećerana: the name of the urban estate in Županja where I lived as a child.

Šećeranci: (Plural) all residents of the estate Kolonija Šećerana, regardless of gender.

Slavonian: a person from Slavonija, Croatia.

Slavonija: Croatian for Slavonia, a historical region of Croatia.

Šokci: a subgroup of Croats but not a separate ethnicity.

Tata: Croatian word for father.

Zagreb: the capital and largest city in Croatia.

Županja: a town in eastern Slavonia, Croatia, located 254 km east of Zagreb.

About the Author

Ruža Dabić-Bučak was born in Croatia in 1950 and grew up in her much loved Kolonija, Ŝećerana, Županja. Ruža and her husband immigrated to Melbourne, Australia, in 1971, where they still live with their two children and three grandchildren.

A retired oncology clinical nurse consultant, Ruža came to poetry late in life, writing her first poems just two days before her 60th birthday. She writes in both English and Croatian.

Petals is Ruža's first collection of poetry.

www.ingramcontent.com/pod-product-compliance
Lightning Source LLC
Chambersburg PA
CBHW060107230426
43661CB00033B/1423/J